P(

Prayers

for

Everyday

Living

A diverse collection of
prayers offering hope,
happiness and wisdom.

Library and Archives Canada Cataloguing in Publication

Powerful prayers for everyday living : a diverse collection of prayers offering hope, happiness and wisdom / [edited by] Mark Linden O'Meara.

Includes some prayers written by Mark Linden O'Meara.
ISBN 978-0-9680459-9-2

   1. Prayers. I. O'Meara, Mark Linden, 1958-
BL560.P692 2009   204'.3   C2009-901775-X

Published by Soul Care Publishing

Cover photo of woman:
Istockphoto.com - Oleg Prikhodko
Cover photo of sunset:
Istockphoto.com - Peeter Viisimaa
Back photo: Blessing by Wang Nengtao, photo by Steve Haavik

Some prayers are attributed to "author unknown." Care has been taken to reproduce only public domain prayers or prayers written by the editor of this book. If you are aware of any corrections to the authorship of a prayer in this book, the publisher would welcome such information.

Dedication...

This book is dedicated to all those who have shown me faith: my wife Sophia, my daughter Samantha, my very good friend Steve who always encourages the creativity in people, and my friends who encouraged me with believing that creating this book was a good idea.

I give gratitude to the builders of Notre Dame Cathedral in Paris, and St. Patrick's Cathedral in Dublin for it was in these places that I had the most remarkable experiences and beginnings.

Thanks to Josee, an angel who gave me a special message to rise up again from adversity.

Thanks to Theresa Pugh for encouragement and ideas, and Julie Cochrane for layout guidance.

About the Author

Mark O'Meara is a true renaissance man who celebrates his creativity through music, writing, video, publishing and comedy. Mark has authored numerous thought provoking articles such as "Healing the Ghosts of Xmas Past" and "The Deeper Health Issues of Anti-Depressants", He has recorded a music CD, written two children's books, published books about China, and has now created a powerful prayer book.

Mark has a Masters degree in Counseling. He began writing his award winning first book "Here I Am" after discovering that tears and laughter were his keys to mental health instead of medication. He wrote the book in hope that others will experience life free from emotional pain.

Mark has become an inspiration to many of his readers by candidly sharing how he overcame his own personal issues. Now he has brought together a powerful and practical prayer book which is certain to become a present day classic.

*Here I Am is published in the USA as "Let Go and Be Happy."

Table of Contents

On Prayer

Prayer is the soul's sincere desire,
uttered or unexpressed;
The motion of a hidden fire,
what trembles in the breast.
Prayer is the burden of a sigh,
the falling of a tear,
the upward glancing of an eye,
when none but God is near.
Prayer is the simplest form of speech
that infant lips can try;
Prayer, the sublimest strains that reach,
the Majesty on high.
Prayer is the contrite sinner's voice
returning from his ways,
while angels in their songs rejoice,
and cry, "Behold, the one who prays!"
Prayer is the believer's vital breath,
the believers native air;
the watchword at the gates of death,
one enters heaven with prayer.

J. Montgomery

The World's Need

So many gods,
so many creeds,
so many paths,
that wind and wind,
while just the art,
of being kind,
is all the sad world needs.
Ella Wheeler Wilcox

Common Prayer of Humanity

In that which we share,
let us see the common prayer of humanity.
In that in which we differ,
let us wonder at the freedom of man.
In our unity and our differences,
let us know the uniqueness that is God.

from Forms of Prayer for Jewish Worship.

The Presence

We are now in the presence of pure being,
and immersed in the Holy Spirit,
of life, love and wisdom.
We acknowledge thy presence,
and thy power, O blessed spirit.
In Thy divine wisdom,
now erase our mortal limitations,
and from Thy pure substance of love,
bring into manifestation,
our world,
according to Thy perfect law.

Unity prayer

A Morning Prayer

Be still and enjoy the quiet time,
and listen between the words,
taking time to bless myself and bless others.
Let my soul speak to me,
allowing God into my vocabulary,
that I may feel the wonder of the miracle of life.
Help me find the way to connect with my compassion,
for compassion will heal the world.
Let me pay attention to the synchronicities,
and to act by taking the next step,
for action with vision brings a new order.
Help me overcome my doubt,
and to doubt my doubt,
and banish all thoughts that I am not enough.
Starting my day with gratitude,
I deeply know that I am not alone,
and that my Angels are always with me.

Mark Linden O'Meara
inspired by Grace Cirocco

Enter the Gate

Peace be unto thee, stranger,
enter and be not afraid.
I have left the gate open,
and thou art welcome to my home.
There is room in my house for all.
I have swept the hearth and lighted the fire.
The room is warm and cheerful,
and you will find comfort and rest within.
The table is laid and the fruits of life
are spread before thee.
The wine is also here,
it sparkles in the light.
I have set a chair for you,
where the sunbeams dance through the shade.
Sit and rest and refresh your soul.
Eat of the fruit and drink the wine.
All, all is yours, and you are welcome.

Ernest Holmes

You

You are wisdom, uncreated and eternal,
the supreme first cause, above all being,
sovereign Godhead, sovereign goodness,
watching unseen the God-inspired
wisdom of your people.
Raise us, we pray, that we may totally respond
to the supreme, unknown, ultimate, and splendid height
of your words, mysterious and inspired.
There all God's secret matters lie covered and hidden
under darkness both profound and brilliant,
silent and wise.
You make what is ultimate and beyond brightness
secretly to shine in all that is most dark.
In your way, ever unseen and intangible,
you fill to the full with most beautiful splendor
those souls who close their eyes that they may see.
And I, please, with love that goes on beyond mind
to all that is beyond mind,
seek to gain such for myself through this prayer.

St. Denis

The Treasure

Pain is a treasure, for it contains mercies.
The kernel is soft when the rind is scraped off.
Oh brother, the place of darkness and cold
is the fountain of life in the cup of ecstasy.
So also is endurance of pain and sickness and disease.
For from abasement proceeds exultation.
The spring seasons are hidden in the autumns.
And the autumns are charged with springs.

Rumi

Beholding Thy Face

When I behold thy peerless face,
beaming with love, oh Lord,
what fear have I of earthly woe,
or of the frown of sorrow?
As the first ray of the dawning sun dispels the dark,
so too Lord, when thy blessed light
bursts forth within the heart,
it scatters all our grief and pain with sweetest balm.
When on thy love and grace I ponder,
in my heart's deepest depths,
tears of joy stream down my cheeks beyond restraining.
Hail gracious lord! Hail gracious One!
I shall proclaim that I love.
May my life-breath depart from me,
as I perform Thy works!

Author unknown

Dance of Bliss

Upon the sea of blissful awareness
ways of ecstatic love arise.
Rapture divine! Play of God's bliss!
Ah! How enthralling!
Wondrous ways of the sweetness of God,
ever new and ever enchanting,
rise on the surface,
ever assuming, forms ever fresh.
Then once more in the great communion,
all are merged.
The barrier walls of time and space
dissolve and vanish.
Dance then, oh mind!
Dance in delight, with hands upraised,
chanting Lord 's holy name.

Author unknown

Prayer of Thanks

I thank you God for this amazing day,
for the leaping greenly spirits of trees,
and a blue true dream of sky,
and for everything which is infinite which is yes.
I who have died come alive again today.
And this is the sun's birthday.
This is the birthday
of life and of love and wings,
and of the great happening,
and illimitable earth.

E. E. Cummings

Self Forgiveness

Whatever evil deeds I have committed
due to passion, aggression, and ignorance,
through body, speech, and likewise mind,
I confess them each and every one.

Buddhist prayer

Perfect Teachings

Perfectly completing the ocean of merit,
completely purifying the ocean of wisdom,
perfectly completing the entire ocean of aspiration,
may all beings become supremely noble,
may the teacher come to the world,
may the teachings shine like the sun,
may the holders of the doctrine,
and the Sangha of students be in harmony,
and may the goodness of the teachings,
remain for a long time.

Buddhist prayer

The Common Wealth

When the perfect order prevails,
the world is like a home shared by all,
the virtuous and worthy are elected to public office,
and the capable hold posts
of gainful employment in society,
peace and trust among all are the maxims of living,
all love and respect their own parents and children
as well as the parents and children of others,
there is caring for the old,
there are jobs for the adults,
there are nourishment and education for the children,
there is a means of support for the widows,
and the widowers,
for all who find themselves alone in the world,
and for the disabled.
Every man and woman has an appropriate role
to play in the family and society.
A sense of sharing displaces the effects
of selfishness and materialism.
A devotion to public duty
leaves no room for idleness.
Intrigues and conniving for ill gain unknown.
Villains such as thieves and robbers do not exist.
The door of every home need never be locked
and bolted by day or night.
These are the characteristics of an ideal world,
the Commonwealth state.

Confucius's Record of Rights Book IX

Forward Looking

My thoughts are creative.
I see positive pictures while reminding myself
about the nature of true and false thoughts.
Seeing the truth, I acknowledge that
I am always learning and there is always hope.
I no longer pre-judge others.
I doubt my doubt.
I no longer fear my fear.
I choose optimism and gratitude.
I listen deeply to others in every sacred moment.
These truths always I apply.

Mark Linden O'Meara
inspired by chapter titles of
No Chance Encounter by K. Pollack

Remembering Compassion

O God, when I have food,
help me to remember the hungry.
When I have work,
help me to remember the jobless.
When I have a home,
help me to remember those
who have no home at all.
When I am without pain,
help me to remember those who suffer.
And remembering,
help me to destroy my complacency.
Bestir my compassion,
and be concerned enough to help.
By word and deed,
those who cry out
for what we take for granted.
Amen.

Samuel F. Pugh

Prayer to Mother Earth

We return thanks to our mother,
the earth, which sustains us.
We return thanks to the rivers and streams,
which supply us with water.
We return thanks to all herbs,
which furnish medicines
for the cure of our diseases.
We return thanks to the corn,
and to her sisters, the beans and squash,
which give us life.
We return thanks to the bushes and trees,
which provide us with fruit.
We return thanks to the wind,
which, moving the air,
has banished diseases.
We return thanks to the moon and the stars,
which have given us their light
when the sun was gone.
We return thanks to our grandfather He-no,
who has given to us his rain.
We return thanks to the sun,
that he has looked upon the earth
with a beneficent eye.
Lastly, we return thanks to the Great Spirit,
in whom is embodied all goodness,
and who directs all things,
for the good of his children.

An Iroquois Prayer

Surrender

Here Lord is my life.
I place it on the altar today.
Use it as you will.

Albert Schweitzer

A Time for Everything

To everything there is a season,
and a time to every purpose
under the heaven.
A time to be born, and a time to die;
A time to plant,
and a time to pluck up that which is planted;
A time to kill, and a time to heal;
A time to break down, and a time to build up;
A time to weep, and a time to laugh;
A time to mourn, and a time to dance;
A time to cast away stones,
and a time to gather stones together;
A time to embrace,
and a time to refrain from embracing;
A time to get, and a time to lose;
A time to keep, and a time to cast away;
A time to rend, and a time to sew;
A time to keep silence, and a time to speak;
A time to love, and a time to hate;
A time of war, and a time of peace.

Ecclesiastes 3:1-8

Watching the Thought

The thought manifests as the word.
The word manifests as the deed.
The deed develops into habit,
And habit hardens into character.
So watch the thought and its ways with care,
and let it spring forth from love,
born out of concern for all beings.

Buddha

The Golden Rule

What is hateful to you,
do not do to your fellow man.
That is the law,
all the rest is commentary.

Lord Mahavira

God Be With Me

God be with me each and every day.
God be with me in each and every way.
God be with me each and every night.
God be with me everlastingly bright.
Let me not forget you.
Let me feel you.
Let me know you.
Let me trust you.
Let me have faith in you.
Let me live, eat and breathe your presence,
into every atom of my being,
even if for just one minute,
one hour, one day, one night,
for I will be eternally grateful,
and spiritually fulfilled.
Let your presence grow in me.
Unshackle me.
What can I do,
to nurture and worship,
your divine presence in me,
in everything?
God, please be with me.

Cory Savitsky

Lead Me

From the unreal, lead me to the real.
From darkness, lead me to light.
From death lead me to immortality.
May all beings dwell in happiness.
May all beings dwell in peace.
May all beings attain oneness.
May all beings attain auspiciousness.
May happiness be unto the whole world.
Om, peace, peace, peace.

Ancient Sanskrit prayer

Being Present

Creator, help me each moment,
to be more in my body,
to be practicing patience and tolerance,
to be fostering an intention of love and kindness,
to be breathing deeply the air of life,
and to be looking inward and outward,
to be finding meaning in all,
and in times of emptiness,
to be filling myself with hope.

Mark Linden O'Meara

Love Is...

Love is self-sufficient.
It is pleasing to itself and on its own account.
Love is its own payment, its own reward.
Love needs no extrinsic cause or result.
Love is the result of love,
it is intrinsically valuable.
I love because I love.
I love in order to love.
Love is a valuable thing,
only if it returns to its beginning,
consults its origin,
and flows back to its source.
It must always draw from the endless stream.
Love is the only one
of the soul's motions, senses, and affections,
by which the creature in his inadequate fashion,
may respond to his Creator,
and pay God back in kind.
When God loves,
God wishes only to be loved in return.
Assuredly God loves for no other purpose
than to be loved.
God knows that those who love God,
are happy in their love.

St. Bernard of Clairvaux

A Prayer for Couples

Love one another,
but make not a bond of love.
Let it rather be a moving sea,
between the shores or your souls.
Fill each other's cup,
but drink not from one cup.
Give one another of your bread,
but eat not from the same loaf.
Sing and dance together and be joyous,
but let each one of you be alone;
even as the strings of a lute are alone,
though they quiver with the same music.
Give your hearts,
but not into each other's keeping,
for only the hand of Life can contain your hearts.
And stand together
yet not too near together;
for the pillars of the temple stand apart,
and the oak tree and the cypress grow
not in each other's shadow.

Kahil Gibran

The Soul of Love

May I be attuned to the confusion
that new ideas bring,
yet graceful in spirit,
to those who hold a different view.
May I be aware that I cannot give to the world,
that which I have not cultivated in myself,
for I have no morally persuasive power,
with those I hold in contempt.
May I always know that Love restores reason,
and that in every human heart is a love,
that can heal all political and social relationships,
and that it is my calling,
to find the soul of love,
in all others and all that I do,
knowing that problems cannot be solved,
on the level of consciousness that created them.
Knowing there is no "us" and no "them",
may I humbly do my part!

Mark Linden O'Meara
inspired by the thoughts of Albert Einstein,
Mahatma Ghandi, Martin Luther King,
Marianne Williamson and
Pierre Theilard de Chardin

Commandments

Kill not, but have regard for life.
Steal not, neither do ye rob.
Abstain from impurity,
and lead a life of chastity.
Lie not, but be truthful.
Speak the truth with discretion,
fearlessly and in a loving heart.
Invent not evil reports,
neither do ye repeat them.
Carp not, but look for,
the good sides of your fellow beings,
so that you may,
with sincerity defend them,
against their enemies.
Swear not, but speak decently and with dignity.
Waste not the time with gossip,
but speak to the purpose or keep silence.
Covet not, nor envy, but rejoice,
at the fortunes of other people.
Cleanse your heart of malice and cherish no hatred,
not even against your enemies,
but embrace all living beings with kindness.
Free your mind of ignorance
and be anxious to learn the truth,
especially in the one thing that is needful,
lest you fall a prey either to skepticism or to errors.
Skepticism will make you indifferent and errors
will lead you astray, so that you shall not find
the noble path that leads to eternal life.

Buddhist Teachings

Now is the Time

Until one is committed,
there is hesitancy,
the chance to draw back,
always ineffectiveness.
Concerning acts of initiative and creation,
there is one elementary truth,
the ignorance of which,
kills countless ideas and splendid plans.
The moment one definitely commits oneself,
then providence moves too.
All sorts of things occur to help one,
that would never otherwise have occurred.
A whole stream of events issues from the decision,
raising in one's favour,
all manner of unforeseen incidents,
and meetings and material assistance,
which no one could have dreamt,
would come one's way.
Whatever you can do,
or dream you can,
Begin it!
Boldness has genius, power,
and magic in it.
Begin it now!

Goethe

Lead Me to Peace

Lead me from death to life,
from falsehood to truth,
from despair to hope,
from fear to trust,
from hate to love,
from war to peace.
Let peace fill our hearts,
our world, our universe.

From St. Patrick's Church,
Dublin, Ireland

Quench My Thirst

O God, you are my god,
I seek you,
my soul thirsts for you,
my flesh faints for you,
as in a dry and weary land
where there is no water.
So I have looked upon you
in the sanctuary,
beholding your power and glory.
Because your steadfast love
is better than life,
my lips will praise you.
So I will bless you as long as I live
I will lift up my hands
and call on your name.
My soul is satisfied as with a rich feast
and my mouth praises you
with joyful lips.
You have been my help,
and in the shadow of your wings,
I sing for joy.
My soul clings to you.
Your right hand upholds me.

Excerpts from Psalm 63

My Life is Inspired

May I be blessed with
a pure romantic gift,
a soaring imagination,
a lyrical impulse,
a passion for freedom,
and a magical spiritual appeal.
May I seek in language,
the spirit and the essence,
to express through my words,
the spirit, mind and body of living.

Mark Linden O'Meara
inspired by the writings of Kahlil Gibran

My Vow of Awareness

Creations are numberless,
I vow to free them.
Delusions are inexhaustible,
I vow to transform them.
Reality is boundless,
I vow to perceive it.
The awakened way
is unsurpassable,
I vow to embody it.

Buddhist prayer

Prayer for a Departing Friend

Good luck, I wish you well,
for all that wishes may be worth.
I hope that love and strength,
are with you for the length of your time on earth.

From A Winter's Tale by Mike Batt

Traveler's Prayer

May your eyes mingle with the sun.
May your breath be merged with the winds.
May the waters of your being mingle with the oceans.
May the ashes become one with the soil.
May you go to the heavens or to the earth,
Whatever your direction may be.

The Vedas

I Am Free

Do not stand at my grave and weep;
I am not there. I do not sleep.
I am a thousand winds that blow.
I am the diamond glints on snow.
I am the gentle autumn's rain.
When you awaken in the morning's hush,
I am the swift uplifting rush
of quiet birds in circled flight.
I am the soft stars that shine at night.
Do not stand at my grave and cry.
I am not there. I did not die.

Author unknown

Prayer of Virtues

Protect me from chaos and confusion
and restore me to good order,
and allow me to travel
where there are few enemies.
Shield me from those
who would exploit my weakness,
and call on my strengths to guide others.
Turning my disadvantages into advantages,
challenge me when I am ready,
but also give periods of rest and joy.
Help me to wisely confront the unwise,
and speedily move into cooperation.
The virtue of prosperity is temperance,
the virtue of adversity is fortitude,
for prosperity doth best discover vice,
but adversity doth best discover virtue.

*Excerpts from the
Essays of Francis Bacon*

My Heart Wishes

Being gracious, and courteous to strangers,
makes me a citizen of the world,
and that my heart is not an island
cut off from other lands,
but a continent that joins to them.
When my heart easily pardons and remits offences,
then my mind is planted above injuries.
In being thankful for the small benefits,
my heart weighs the good, not the vices.
In the perfection of love,
my heart wishes for salvation of my brethren,
and to move towards the divine nature of life.

Mark Linden O'Meara
inspired by writings of Francis Bacon

Free to Choose

We are the spirit children of God.
We are free to choose good over evil,
exaltation over misery.
God wants us to grow forever,
in light, truth and happiness.
We can demonstrate and strengthen our faith,
through righteous work.
As my understanding increases,
so does my accountability and responsibility.
We make atonement effectively in our lives,
through sincere repentance.
My life is a gift from God,
to enjoy according to God's wisdom,
and my faithfulness.
We have agency to choose good or evil,
but we cannot choose,
the consequences of our choices.
I prepare for eternal life by daily learning,
improving and building the kingdom of God.

Teachings of Brigham Young

Finding You

Help me to find you,
should my thoughts and energies,
become dispersed.
Guide me back
to your teachings,
to be serene,
self-controlled,
and compassionate,
centered and in alliance,
with your love.

Mark Linden O'Meara

A Family Gathering

Grateful for our gathering,
we ask that you favor our family,
with multiplying happiness.
Protect our children,
give grace to our elders,
as we give thanks to our ancestors,
for their blessings.
We gather in their name,
and in the names of our descendants.
Bless us with luck,
and ensure safety for our family.
We petition for these blessings,
in the past, present and future,
as witnesses to your wisdom,
and compassionate vision.

Author unknown

Bring Forth The Day

The golden rays of the rising sun,
illuminate life in the five directions.
Awakening the earth to its joyful ways
I begin my day in trust and happiness,
Bringing forth in my day, friendship, safety,
and prosperity of mind, body and soul.

Author unknown

A Potlatch Prayer

The Power on high doth make me dance.
The Power on high doth make me sing.
The Power on high doth make me play.
The Power on high
doth make me show my ritual,
because wealth, it is in my house.

George Clutesi

I Ask for Forgiveness

Do Thou forgive me, O Lord,
for all my sins committed,
with my hands, feet, speech,
body, ears, eyes, and mind,
while doing actions,
enjoined or otherwise?
Glory unto Thee,
O Thou beneficent,
Thou God of gods,
Thou ocean of mercy.

Ancient Sanskrit prayer

The Tao

The greatest good is like water:
it benefits all life without being noticed.
It flows even to the lowliest places
where no one chooses to be
and so it is very close to the Tao.
It settles only in quiet locations.
Its deepest heart is always clear.
It offers itself with great goodness.
It keeps its rhythm as it keeps its promises.
It governs tributaries as it governs its people.
It adapts to all necessities.
It moves at the right moment.
It never flaunts its goodness
and so it never attracts any blame.

Tao Te Ching: Chapter 8,
translated by Chao-Hsiu Chen

A Prayer of Struggle

I felt my soul was torn,
by the struggle raging within,
and of love my being was shorn,
as I gaze on the pleasures of sin.
Deep in my heart I pondered.
"Do I always struggle alone?"
"Am I like others?" I wondered,
"By life's harsh blasts ever blown."
Then passed like a flash,
through my memory,
a picture of Galilee.
I saw those fishermen,
weary battling a raging sea,
and I heard the voice of the Master,
with peace their souls instill,
dispel their fears of disaster,
and bid the wind and waves be still.
And now, mid the roaring tempest,
when Life's storms break over my soul,
when round me all is darkness,
and lashing waters roll,
when the gales of passion would sway me,
then Master may I hear thee,
bid the storm in my heart be still.

W.E. O'Meara Sr.

Wholeness

One who knows the masculine,
and yet keeps to the feminine,
will become a channel,
drawing all the world toward it.
Being a channel of the world,
they will not be severed,
from the eternal virtue.
And then they can return again,
to the state of infancy.
One who knows the white,
and yet keeps to the black,
will become a standard to the world.
Being the standard of the world,
with them eternal virtue will never falter.
One who knows honor,
and yet keeps to humility,
will become a valley of the world.
With them eternal virtue will be complete,
and then they can return again to wholeness.
Wholeness when divided will make vessels of utility.
These when employed by the Sage,
will become officials and chiefs,
however for a great function,
no discrimination is needed.

From the Tao Te Ching

Prayer to a Child's Nurse

For the long nights you lay awake,
and watched over my unworthy sake,
for your most comfortable hand,
that led me through the uneven land,
for all the story books you read,
for all the pains you comforted,
for all you pitied, all you bore,
in sad and happy days of yore,
my second mother, my first wife,
the angel of my infant life,
from the sick child now well and old,
take nurse, the little book you hold,
and grant it heaven that all who read,
may find as dear a nurse at need.
And every child who lisps my rhyme,
in the bright fireside nursery clime,
may hear it in as kind a voice,
as made my childish days rejoice.

Robert Louis Stevenson

Prayer for Protection

The light of God surrounds us.
The love of God enfolds us.
The power of God protects us.
The presence of God watches over us.
Wherever we are, God is.

James Dillet Freeman

Illumination of Shadows

God, the creator of our being,
help me to be open to a greater insight,
of why we are here,
and why we are here together.
May I become aware of the deceiving mind,
That has fixed ideas and resistance to truth.
Let my spirit evolve in this world.
and let the epiphanies come through.
Remind me that bright light,
illuminates what is hidden,
but also can cast deep shadows,
and that sudden illumination
of possibilities and insight,
can confuse me and leave my mind weak.
Help me to reconcile the light and shadows,
to live kindly, aware and grounded,
and to harness the energy of illumination,
slowly, solidly, healthily, and wisely,
in rising consciousness.

Mark Linden O'Meara
inspired by Kathryn Anderson

Humbleness

Incline us Oh God!
to think humbly of ourselves,
to be severe
only in the examination
of our own conduct,
to consider our fellow-creatures
with kindness,
and to judge of all they say and do
with that charity
which we would desire
from them ourselves.

Jane Austen

Prayer of Focus

Sometimes I find it hard Lord,
to sit and listen to you.
My anger gets in the way,
and my mind crisscrosses
with nasty thoughts.
Help me to share my anger with you,
and not to let it swallow me up.
Help me not to make
other people angry with me,
but show me how to be loving

Timothy King

The Lotus Prayer

By this merit may all attain omniscience.
May it defeat the enemy, wrongdoing.
From the stormy waves of birth,
old age and death,
from the ocean of samsara,
may I free all beings.
By the confidence of the awake,
and compassionate world,
may the lotus garden of wisdom bloom.
May the dark ignorance
of sentient beings be dispelled.
May all beings enjoy
profound and brilliant glory.

Buddhist invocation

Keeper of the Key

Is there some problem in your life to solve,
some passage seeming full of mystery?
God knows, who brings the hidden things to light.
God keeps the key.
Is there some door closed by the Creator's hand,
which widely opened you had hoped to see?
Trust God and wait – for when God shuts the door,
God keeps the key.
Is there some earnest prayer unanswered yet,
or answered not as you had thought 'twould be?
God will make clear your purpose by-and-by.
God keeps the key.
Have patience with your God, your patient God,
all wise, all knowing, no long tarrier God be,
And of the door of all thy future life.
God keeps the key.
Unfailing comfort, sweet and blessed rest,
to know of every door God keeps the key.
That God at last when just God sees 'tis best,
will give it Thee.

Author unknown

A Song of Hope

Silently, music fills my heart.
Songs born of nature enter my soul,
soft as the dew which greets the dawn;
gentle as a soft summer sun dreaming.
Tunes soft as dew pearls, glistening,
fill me with gently glowing music;
Lift me to happiness and joy,
or waken feelings deep in my soul.
Moonlight and dewdrops conjuring,
fill me with songs which linger unforgotten,
singing a morning-song of hope returning,
as I greet the new dawn;
A song of hope,
for a new day dawning.

Viteslav Halek (English version
by Jon Washburn)

What We Can Be

All people are caught
in an inescapable network
of mutuality,
tied in a single garment
of destiny.
Whatever affects one directly,
affects all indirectly.
I can never be what I ought to be
Until you are what you ought to be,
And you can never be
what you ought to be,
until I am what I ought to be.

Martin Luther King, Jr.

Prayer of Purpose

We are each of us divine essence,
placed on earth to create
the good, the true, and the beautiful.
May I be motivated to higher heights,
and to utilize my God-given talents,
in the presence of honor and respect.
My spirit within compels me,
to serve each other rather than compete,
to bless each other rather than condemn,
and to place my primary attention
on the extension of brotherly and sisterly love.
My consciousness now is attuned to love
of the entire human race.
In a surge of energy,
my subconscious is intent
upon abundant joyful life.
My Love is contagious,
and My love has ultimate authority
over the forces of the world.
It proceeds in spite of all obstruction.
Every day, like the inevitable dawn,
more spiritual light seeps into the world.

Mark Linden O'Meara
inspired by Marianne Williamson's
Healing the Soul of America

A Wedding Prayer

May we be made friends
and provide each other nourishment.
May we give each other strength.
May we bring each other prosperity.
May we give each other happiness.
May we bring each other creativity.
May we give each other compassion.
May we bring each other into every life season.
May we keep our relationship steadfast and binding.

Hindu Wedding Tradition

One Who Knows

One who knows others is wise.
One who knows himself is enlightened.
One who conquers others is strong.
One who conquers himself is mighty.
One who knows contentment is rich.
One who keeps on course with energy has will.
One who does not deviate
from the proper place will long endure.
One who may die but not perish has longevity.

*A Zen Master, adapted from
a compilation by Robert May*

Arising

Through me,
In me,
With me,
In the unity
of mind, body and soul,
All love,
compassion and optimism
arises from within.

Mark Linden O'Meara
inspired by Christian prayers

Love

Love is patient and kind.
Love is not jealous or conceited.
Love is not proud or selfish.
Love is not ill mannered.
Love does not hold a grudge.
Love is not happy with evil.
Love is happy with the truth.
Love never gives up.
Love is faith, hope and patient.
Love never fails.

I Corinthians 13:47

Prayer of Worship

Om, We worship Thee,
O sweet Lord of transcendental vision.
O giver of prosperity to all,
may we be free
from the bonds of death,
like a ripe fruit dropping from the tree.
May we never again forget our immortal nature.

Ancient Sanskrit prayer

The Names of God

In your honor God,
I repeat these words daily.
You are
creator, sanctuary, compassion, mercy, emperor, pure, the keeper,
protector, compeller, greatness, the planner, separator, forgiver,
provider, sustenance, opener, learned, dispenser, vanquisher, raiser,
bestower, hearer, all-seeing, arbitrator, judge, awareness, gentle,
magnificent, pardoner, appreciative, venerable, greatest, watchful,
guardian, reckoner, listener, comprehender, wise, beloved, glorious,
resurrector, witness, truth, advocate, powerful, sturdy, friend, auditor,
originator, restorer, quickener, taker, alive, self-subsisting, finder,
noble, unique, peerless, eternal, able, prevailing, bringer, deferrer, first,
last, manifestor, hidden, governor, exhalted, highest, benefactor,
gracious, sovereign, bounteous, equitable, assembler, enriching,
withholder, conferrer, radiant, guide, unseen, everlasting, inheritor,
director, patient, giver, awarder, closest, revealer, sufficient, truthful,
supporter, fountain, answerer, omnipotent, ancient, unwavering,
steadfast, master, blessing, merciful, benign, sincere, abundant, strong,
open-handed, judgment, beautiful, purist, concealing, swift,
omniscient, just, ruler, generous, controlling, knowing, merciful, all-
encompassing, ample, evident, holy, curing, wise, favorable, un-
comparable, supernatural, omnipresent, praiseworthy.

Names of Allah

Optimist's Creed

I promise myself to be so strong
that nothing can disturb my peace of mind;
To talk health, happiness and prosperity
to every person I meet;
To make all my friends feel
that there is something in them;
To look at the sunny side of everything
and make my optimism come true;
To think only of the best,
to work only for the best
and expect only the best;
To be just as enthusiastic
about the success of others
as I am about my own;
To forget the mistakes of the past and press on
to the greater achievements of the future;
To wear a cheerful countenance at all times
and give every living creature I meet a smile;
To give so much time to the improvement of myself
that I have no time to criticize others;
To be too large for worry, too noble for anger,
too strong for fear, and too happy
to permit the presence of trouble.

Adapted from Optimist Creed
by Christian Larson

Wedding Prayer of Shelter

Now you will feel no rain,
for each of you will be shelter to the other.
Now you will feel no cold,
for each of you will be warmth to the other.
Now there is no more loneliness,
for each of you will be companion to the other.
Now you are two bodies,
but there is only one life before you.
Go now to your dwelling place
to enter into the days of your togetherness.
May your days be good and long upon the earth.

Apache Wedding Prayer

Liberation

May I be liberated peacefully,
with the virtuous subduing of my demons.
My spirit becomes unlimited,
and blooms into eternity.

Author unknown

Cultivating Myself

I avoid pride and greed,
always expressing thanks.
I confess my sins,
do charitable deeds,
learn the proper ways,
wishing that all beings will be blessed,
with the elimination of ignorance,
and achievement of true and lasting
wealth and happiness.

Author unknown

A Sikh Prayer

Lord, teach us to make peace
with all that surrounds us.
May we reflect on the meaning
and shape of our universe and nurture it
with prayer, sacrifice and inspirations of great souls.
May our labors and prayers converge
to create a beautiful canopy of dignity,
equality, justice and friendship,
for all living beings,
under the heavens,
to live and prosper in peace.
May the entire creation
move forward in solidarity,
oneness of spirit and purpose,
and together shape and inherit
a legacy worthy of God and man,
where peace is not a dream but our true destiny.

Sikh Prayer

In The Name of God

In the Name of God,
Most Gracious, Most Merciful
O mankind!
We created you from
a single soul, male and female,
and made you into nations and tribes,
so that you may come to know one another.
Truly, the most honored of you
in God's sight is the greatest of you in piety.
God is All-Knowing, All-Aware

Muslim Prayer

Be

Close your eyes and you will see clearly.
Cease to listen and you will hear truth.
Be silent and your heart will sing.
Seek no contacts and you will find union.
Be still and you will move forward on the tide of spirit.
Be gentle and you will need no strength.
Be patient and you will achieve all things.
Be humble and you will remain entire.

Taoist Meditation

The Healing Journey

May all have compassion,
on those who are passing,
through illness and pain,
emotional or physical.
Uphold their spirit,
that they may trust and not be afraid,
and give them the comfort of strength,
on their healing journey.

From St. Patrick's Cathedral,
Dublin Ireland

Angels in our Midst

Sometimes someone I have briefly met,
says something that stir up inside me,
a desire, a rekindling of dreams, my sense of purpose.
They come in human form,
as people, as expressions of God.
They are real people.
And through circumstances, you are helped,
especially in times of confusion.
But even if you follow their advice,
things may not turn out as you wish,
but in the divine will of the creator.
In following creation's guidance,
you will experience your unique lesson,
A life altering lesson!
Angels do exist.
Each of us, with all our troubles,
possess a divineness that at times will
appear to others as an angel's message.
Recognize the angels among us,
not as lofty dreams,
but as expressed through One another.

Mark Linden O'Meara

Compassion

I am because we are.
We are the image of love.
God is in all of us.
Help each other.
Accept one another.
Encourage each other.
Give courage to one another.
To do so is a manifestation
of God's love on earth.

Mark Linden O'Meara

One

This ritual is One.
The food is One.
We who offer the food are One.
The fire of hunger is also One.
All action is One.
We who understand this are One.

Hindu Blessing

Protect My Family

For whom every family
in heaven and on earth is named,
I entrust to your living care,
the members of my family,
both near and far.
Supply their needs,
guide their footsteps,
keep them in safety
of body and soul,
and may peace rest on them,
and all of our loved ones,
for their sake alone,
as I ask,
nothing in return.

From St. Patricks Cathedral,
Dublin Ireland

The Gift of Children

Let us bring the child back.
The child is God's gift to the family.
Each child is created in the special image
and likeness of God
for greater things
to love and to be loved.
We must bring the child
back to the center
of our care and concern.
This is the only way that
our world can survive,
because our children,
are the only hope for the future.
As other people are called to God,
only their children can take their places.

Mother Teresa

Forgiveness Prayer

Creator, help me,
forgive them their trespasses for at times,
they know not what they do.
Creator, help me,
forgive my parents, for at times,
they know not what they do.
Creator, help me,
forgive my brothers and sisters, for at times,
they know not what they do.
Creator, help me,
forgive those who have harmed me, for at times,
they know not what they do.
Creator, help me,
forgive myself, for at times,
I know not what I do.

Mark Linden O'Meara

Ruthlessness

Help me be ruthless,
ruthlessly compassionate
with myself,
ruthlessly compassionate
with others.

Mark Linden O'Meara

All is Yours

All life is your own,
All fruits of the earth
are fruits of your womb,
your union, your dance.
Lady and lord,
we thank you for
blessings and abundance.
Join with us, feast with us,
enjoy with us!

*Traditional Native
American prayer*

Opportunity

Often has opportunity been missed,
because it was dressed in overalls,
and looked like work!
Be not regretful though
of what you have missed.
God will come calling again.

Adapted from writings
of Thomas Emerson

Vulnerability

Let me be free,
to meet your lasting gaze,
to be free of thoughts,
to let your eyes meet mine,
without self consciousness,
only consciousness of self.
Let me be free of my mind and feelings,
of words that need not be spoken,
that would only hide my fear,
of exposing the inner me.
Let me share myself,
without judgment.
I am neither a good person,
nor am I bad.
I am just, a person.
One of many,
many of the One.

Mark Linden O'Meara

May My Right
Prayer Be First

I prayed for riches and achieved success,
all that I touched turned into gold. Alas!
My cares were greater, and my peace was less
when that wish came to pass.
I prayed for glory; and heard my name
sung by sweet children and by hoary men.
But ah! the hurts, the hurts that came with fame!
I was not happy then.
I prayed for love, and had my soul's desire,
through quivering heart and body and through brain
there swept the flame of its devouring fire;
and there the scars remain.
I prayed for a contented mind. At length
great light upon my darkened spirit burst,
great peace fell on me, also, and great strength.
Oh! Had that prayer been first!

Ella Wheeler Wilcox

Creatures of
the Earth

Know other creatures' love for life,
for they are like you.
Kill them not.
Save their life from fear and enmity.
All creatures desire to live, not to die,
hence to kill is to sin.
A godly man does not kill.
Therefore, kill not yourself,
consciously or unconsciously,
living organisms which
move or move not,
nor cause slaughter of them.
He who looketh on the creatures
of the earth, big and small, as his own self,
comprehendeth this immense world.
Among the careless, he who restraineth self
is enlightened.

Jain Prayer of non-violence

Breaking of Bread

Bless our hearts,
to hear in the breaking of bread,
the song of the universe.

Benedictine Blessing

Countless Blessings

When you rise in the morning,
give thanks for the light,
for your life, for your strength.
Give thanks for your food and for the joy of living.
If you see no reason to give thanks,
the fault lies in yourself.
We give thanks for all your countless blessings,
for each new morning with its light,
for rest and shelter of the night,
for health and food,
for love and friends,
for everything thy goodness sends.

Tecumseh (Shawnee chief)
and Ralph Waldo Emerson

May There Be Peace

May there be peace in heaven.
May there be peace in the sky.
May there be peace on earth.
May there be peace in the water.
May there be peace in the plants.
May there be peace in the trees.
May there be peace in the gods.
May there be peace in the Absolute God.
May there be peace in all.
May that peace, real peace, be mine.

Ancient Sanskrit prayer

Prayer of St Francis
of Assisi

Lord,

make me an instrument of your peace.

Where there is hatred, let me sow love;

where there is injury, pardon;

where there is doubt, faith;

where there is despair, hope;

where there is darkness, light;

where there is sadness, joy.

O Divine Master,

grant that I may not so much seek

to be consoled, as to console;

to be understood, as to understand;

to be loved, as to love.

For it is in giving that we receive;

it is in pardoning that we are pardoned;

And it is in the death of selfishness,

that we awaken to eternal life.

St. Francis of Assisi
The original last two lines were
"and it is in dying that we are born to eternal life."
The interpretation of these two
lines is attributed to Norman Lear

Whatever Your Troubles Be

Whoever you are as you read this
whatever your trouble or grief,
I want you to know and to heed this:
The day draweth near with relief.
No sorrow, no woe is unending,
though heaven seems voiceless and dumb;
So sure as your cry is ascending,
so surely an answer will come.
Whatever temptation is near you,
whose eyes on this simple verse fall;
Remember good angels will hear you
and help you to stand, if you call.
Though stunned with despair I beseech you,
whatever your losses, your need,
believe, when these printed words reach you,
believe you were born to succeed.
You are stronger, I tell you, this minute,
than any unfortunate fate!
And the coveted prize — you can win it!
While life lasts 'tis never too late!

Ella Wheeler Wilcox

The Twelve Soul Powers

I have absolute faith in God the Good.
I am strong and unafraid.
I am loving and I am loved.
I am guided into wise and right action.
I see new and creative ways of doing what is mine to do.
My thoughts and words vibrate with power.
I see to the heart of things and I know what to do.
I am willing to fulfill my soul's higher purpose.
I am filled with creative new energy.
Divine order and divine timing are established
in my mind, body and affairs.
I release all false and limited beliefs,
and anything that is a distraction,
to my spiritual unfoldment.
Every cell in my body,
is now being charged,
with the pure restorative life of God.

Adapted from Unity Prayer

Prayer of St. Columba

My dearest lord,
be thou a bright flame before me,
be thou a smooth path beneath me,
be though a kindly shepherd behind me,
today and forever more.

St. Columba

Prayer to St. Therese

Teach us to follow,
in your way,
of confidence and trust.
Help us to realize that God's love,
watches over us each day of our lives.
Obtain for us the light to see,
in sorrow and in joy,
in trials as in peace,
the loving hand of God.
Give us your faith and trust,
so that we may walk,
in darkness as in the light,
holding fast to the way of love,
knowing as you did,
that everything is a grace.

St. Therese

Revealed

No eye has seen,
no ear has heard,
no mind has conceived,
what God has prepared,
for those who love God.
But God has revealed it to us by his Spirit.
The Spirit searches all things,
even the deep things of God.

I Corinthinans 2 9-10

Asking

Call to me,
and I will answer you,
and I will tell you
great and mighty things,
which you do not know.

Jeremiah 33:3

God's Heartbeat

God is indiscriminate.
God does not judge.
God is in the child.
God is in the adult.
God is in our heart.
God is in our mind.
God is in our word.
God is in our song.
God is in you.
God is in me.
Let me be pure,
and see the God in all,
including those I might call sinners,
so that I may be wooed,
to the call of love,
and hear God's heartbeat.

Author unknown

No More Than Now

There was never any more inception,
than there is now;
Nor any more youth or age,
than there is now;
And will never be any more perfection,
than there is now;
Nor any more heaven or hell,
than there is now....
Clear and sweet is my soul,
and clear and sweet is,
all that is not my soul.

Walt Whitman

Prayer for the Learner

May I be granted the power of faith,
to believe in the ability of my teachers,
and that my teachers will convey the truth.
May I be granted the power of conscientiousness,
that I may have a sense of conscience
when acting wrongly in thought word or deed.
May I be granted the power of fear,
so that I may fear the blame of acting wrongly,
in thought word or deed.
May I be granted the power of discernment,
that I may have the energy to discard wrong things
and adopt the right ones.
May I be granted the power of insight,
so that I may understand the real nature of things.

Mark Linden O'Meara
inspired by the teachings of the Buddha

The Hand of the Eternal

But ask the beasts, and they will teach you;
the birds of the sky, and they will tell you;
or speak to the earth and it will teach you.
Who among all of these does not know,
that the hand of the Eternal has done this?

Job 12:7-9

Invocation for Health and Longevity

I am strong; the sky is clear.
I am strong; the earth is stable.
I am strong; men are at peace with one another.
I am supported by the harmony of all three spheres.
All of my spiritual elements return to me.
The yin and yang of my life-being,
are well integrated.
My life root is firm.
As I follow the path of revitalization,
my mind and emotions,
become wholesomely active.
The goddess of my heart
nourishes my life abundantly.
Internal Chi enhances my spiritual growth,
and all obstacles dissolve before me.
The channels of my life energy are balanced.
My natural healing power,
contributes to a long and happy life,
so that my virtuous fulfillment in the world,
can be accomplished.
By following the subtle law,
and integral way of life,
I draw ever closer,
to the divine realm of the Subtle Origin.

Ni, Hua-Ching

Psalm 23

You, Lord, are my shepherd.
I will never be in need.
You let me rest
in fields of green grass.
You lead me to streams
of peaceful water,
and you refresh my life.
You are true to your name,
and you lead me
along the right paths.
I may walk through valleys
as dark as death,
but I won't be afraid.
You are with me,
and your shepherd's rod,
makes me feel safe.
You treat me to a feast,
while my enemies watch.
You honor me as your guest,
and you fill my cup
until it overflows.
Your kindness and love
will always be with me
each day of my life,
and I will live forever
in your house, Lord.

Contemporary English Version,
American Bible Society

Springtime

Now is the springtime,
and the bounty of heaven,
is pouring on earth and the fields,
and rose gardens are in growth,
and development.
Exert yourself as much as thou can,
in order that through this everlasting bounty,
and the sprinklings of the divine gift,
thou may grow and thrive,
like unto a fruitful tree,
with the utmost freshness and purity.

Abdu'l –Baha

Being Together

Thank you,
for the wind and rain,
and sun and pleasant weather.
Thank you for this our food,
and that we are together.

Mennonite blessing

The Serenity Prayer

God grant me the serenity
to accept the things I cannot change;
the courage to change the things I can;
and wisdom to know the difference.
Living one day at a time;
Enjoying one moment at a time;
Accepting hardships as the pathway to peace;
Taking, as He did, this sinful world
as it is, not as I would have it;
Trusting that He will make all things right
if I surrender to God's Will;
That I may be reasonably happy in this life
and supremely happy with God
Forever in the next.
Amen.

Reinhold Neibuhr
(masculine words such as "He" and "Him"
have been replaced with the word "God")

Peace Within You

May today there be peace within you.
May you trust your highest power,
that you are right where you are meant to be.
May you not forget the infinite possibilities
that are born of faith.
May you use those gifts that you have received,
and pass on the love that has been given to you.
May you be content knowing
you are a child of God.
Let this presence settle into our bones,
and allow your soul,
the freedom to sing, dance,
and to bask in the sun.
It is there for each and every one of you.

Author unknown

We are Already One

My dear brothers and sisters,
we are already one,
but we imagine that we are not.
What we have to recover is our original unity.
What we have to become is what we already are.

Thomas Merton

Be This

Be generous in prosperity,
and thankful in adversity.
Be worthy of the trust of thy neighbor,
and look upon him with
a bright and friendly face.
Be a treasure to the poor,
an admonisher to the rich,
an answer of the cry of the needy,
a preserver of the sanctity of thy pledge.
Be fair in thy judgment,
and guarded in thy speech.
Be unjust to no man,
and show all meekness to all men.
Be as a lamp unto them
that walk in darkness,
a joy to the sorrowful,
a sea for the thirsty,
a haven for the distressed,
an upholder and defender
of the victim of oppression.
Let integrity and uprightness
distinguish all thine acts.
Be a home for the stranger,
a balm to the suffering,
a tower of strength for the fugitive.
Be eyes to the blind,
and a guiding light,
unto the feet of the erring.

*Gleanings from the
Writings of Baha'u'llah*

Diffusion

That I may reach that purest heaven,
be to other souls the cup of strength
in some great agony,
enkindle generous ardor, feed pure love,
be the sweet presence of a good diffused,
and in diffusion ever more intense!
So shall I join the choir invisible
whose music is the gladness of the world.

George Eliot

Decide to Forgive

Decide to forgive
for resentment is negative,
resentment is poisonous,
resentment diminishes
and devours the self.
Be the first to forgive,
to smile and to take the first step,
and you will see happiness bloom
on the face of your human brother or sister.
Be always the first.
Do not wait for others to forgive,
for by forgiving
you become the master of fate,
the fashioner of life,
the doer of miracles.
To forgive is the highest,
most beautiful form of love.
In return you will receive
untold peace and happiness.

Robert Muller

Achieving a Truly Forgiving Heart

Sunday: Forgive yourself.
Monday: Forgive your family.
Tuesday: Forgive your friends and associates.
Wednesday: Forgive across economic lines
within your own nation.
Thursday: Forgive across cultural lines
within your own nation.
Friday: Forgive across political lines
within your own nation.
Saturday: Forgive other nations.
Only the brave know how to forgive.
A coward never forgives.
It is not in his nation.

Robert Muller

Finding a Soul Mate

I am alone but not lonely.
I pray that the divine order,
will bring to me a special friend,
at the time and place,
anointed with the synchronicity,
of the Creator.
At that time of knowing,
I will have learned lessons,
needed to be learned,
Yet this person will help me embark,
on a new journey,
of togetherness,
and the knowing,
of my soul's many ages.

Mark Linden O'Meara

Relax

Drop thy still dews of quietness,
till all our strivings cease.
Take from our souls the strains and stress,
and let our ordered lives confess,
the beauty of Thy Peace.

John Greenleaf Whittier

Lord is All Around

Go before us to lead us,
Behind us to prompt us,
Under us to support us,
Above us to bless us,
Around us to protect us.
Come within us that we may serve you,
with body and soul and mind,
to the glory of your name.

Nathan Soderblom

A Hindu Prayer

May there be welfare to all beings.
May there be fullness and wholeness to all people.
May there be constant good
and auspicious life to everyone.
May there be peace everywhere.
May all be full of happiness and abundance.
May everyone in the world enjoy,
complete health, free from diseases.
May all see and experience,
good things in their lives.
May not even a single person,
experience sorrow and misery.
Om! Peace! Peace! Peace!

Daily Hindu Prayer

Lift Your Hands

When you lift your hands,
outspread in prayer,
I will hide my eyes from you.
Though you offer countless prayers,
I will not listen.
There is blood on your hands....
Cease to do evil,
learn to do right,
pursue justice and
champion the oppressed.
Give the orphan his rights,
plead the widow's cause.

Isaiah 1:15-17

Seeing Beyond Today

If we could see beyond today,
as God can see,
if all the clouds should roll away,
the shadows flee.
Over present griefs we would not fret,
each sorrow we should soon forget,
for many joys are waiting yet,
for you and me.
If we could know beyond today,
as God does know,
why dearest treasures pass away
and tears must flow
and why the darkness leads to light
why dreary paths will soon grow bright.
Someday life's wrongs will be made right.
Faith tells us so.
If we could see, if we could know,
we often say,
that God in love a veil does throw,
across our way.
We cannot see what lies before,
and so we cling to God the more.
God leads us,
Trust and obey.

Chas Cowman

Love is

Love is the most great law,
that ruleth this mighty and heavenly cycle,
the unique power, that bindeth together,
the diverse elements of this material world,
the supreme magnetic force
that directeth the movements of the spheres
in the celestial realms.
Love revealeth
with unfailing and limitless power,
the mysteries latent in the universe.
Love is the spirit of life,
unto the adorned body of mankind,
the establisher of true civilization
in this mortal world,
and the shedder of imperishable glory,
upon every high-aiming race and nation.

Selections from the
Writings of Abdu'l-Baha

Words of Wisdom

That which is most needed is a loving heart.
May I be aware when my heart is loving,
and when it is not.
To serve the wise,
and not to serve the foolish,
is the greatest blessing.
May I be able to discern the wise,
from the foolish,
without judgment of either.
Those are happy, who avoid,
both victory and defeat.
May I relinquish my need for victory,
and be lifted from feelings of defeat.
When a tree is burning,
how can birds live in it?
Free me from my passions,
so that truth may live in my tree.
People are ashamed of
what they need not be ashamed,
yet are not ashamed of
what they should be ashamed of.
Help me to develop
a healthy concept of shame,
forever forgiving myself,
yet aware of my thoughts,
words and deeds,
so that no harm may come,
to myself or others.
The Buddha shows the way,
but it is I that must make the effort.

Mark Linden O'Meara
inspired by words of the Bhudda

Rendering Peaceful

May there be peace on earth,
peace in the atmosphere,
and in the heavens.
Peaceful be the waters,
the herbs and plants.
May the Divine bring us Peace.
May the holy prayers,
and invocations of peace-liturgies
generate ultimate
Peace and Happiness everywhere.
With these meditations,
which resolve and dissolve
harm, violence, and conflicts,
we render peaceful,
whatever on earth is terrible,
sinful, cruel, and violent.
Let the earth become fully auspicious.
Let everything be beneficial to us.

Athara-Veda XIX-9

My Daily Question

What good can I do today?

Benjamin Franklin's question
to himself every morning

Lead Us

O Lord, lead us from the unreal to the real,
Lead us from darkness to light,
And lead us from death to immortality.
May all be free from dangers.
May all realize what is good.
May all be actuated by noble thoughts.
May all rejoice everywhere. May all be happy.
May all be free from disease.
May all realize what is good.
May none be subject to misery.
May the wicked become virtuous,
may the virtuous attain tranquility.
May the tranquil be free from bonds.
May the freed make others free.
May good betide all people.
May the sovereign righteously rule the earth.
May all beings ever attain what is good.
May the worlds be prosperous and happy.
May the clouds pour rain in time.
May the earth be blessed with crops.
May all countries be freed from calamity.
May holy men live without fear.
May the Lord, the destroyer of sins,
the presiding deity
of all sacred works, be satisfied.
For, God being pleased,
the whole universe becomes pleased.
God being satisfied,
the whole universe feels satisfied.

Swami Yatiswarandanda

Circumstances

Teach me, God, so to use,
all the circumstances of my life today,
that they may bring forth in me,
the fruits of holiness rather than the fruits of sin.
Let me use disappointments as material for patience.
Let me use success as material for thankfulness.
Let me use suspense as material for perseverance.
Let me use danger as material for courage.
Let me use reproach as material for longsuffering.
Let me use praise as material for humility.
Let me use pleasure as material for temperance.
Let me use pains as material for endurance.

John Baillie

Prayer for Good Thoughts

Notice the power of your mind,
to create what you desire.
It is time to turn your thoughts,
to creating inside yourself,
the images, sensations, thoughts and feelings,
of the things you want in life,
of serenity, love joy and companionship,
so that your new inner world,
becomes your new outer world.
All of this exists within your infinite space of mind.
Let your mind grasp the depths of space,
from which you can create.
You are your own universe.
Others are universes too.
Let's see what we can create together!

Mark Linden O'Meara

Long Enduring

Fame or your person,
which is nearer to you?
Your person or wealth,
which is dearer to you?
Gain or loss,
which brings more evil to you?
Over-love of anything,
will lead to wasteful spending.
Amassed riches will be followed,
by heavy plundering.
Therefore, One who knows contentment,
can never be humiliated.
One who knows where to stop,
can never be perishable.
They will long endure.

Lao Tzu

An Indian Prayer (Part I }

Oh Great Spirit,
whose voice I hear in the wind and,
whose breath gives life to all the world,
hear me.
I am weak and small,
and I need your strength and wisdom.
Let me walk in beauty,
and let my eyes ever behold,
the red and purple sunset.
Make my hands always respect,
the things you have made,
and my ears sharp to hear your voice.
Make me wise so that I may understand,
the things you have taught my people.
Let me learn the lessons,
you have hidden in every leaf and rock.
I seek your strength, not to be greater,
than my brother or sister,
but to fight my greatest enemy, myself.
Make me always ready to come to you
with clean hands and sharp eyes,
so that when life fades as the fading sunset,
my spirit may come to you without shame.

An Indian Prayer (Part II)

Great Spirit of Love, come to me,
with the power of the North.
Make me courageous,
when the cold winds of life fall upon me.
Give me strength and endurance,
for everything that is harsh,
everything that hurts,
and everything that makes me flinch.
Make me move through life,
ready to take everything,
that comes from the North.

An Indian Prayer (Part III)

Spirit who comes out of the East,
come to me,
with the power of the rising sun.
Let there be delight in my work.
Let there be light on the path that I walk.
Let me always remember,
that you give the gift of a new day.
Never let me be burdened,
with sorrow by not starting over.

An Indian Prayer (Part IV)

Great Spirit of Creation,
send me the warm and soothing winds,
from the South.
Comfort me and caress me,
when I am tired and cold.
Unfold me like your gentle breezes,
unfold your leaves on the trees,
and as you give to the earth,
your warm, soothing winds,
give to me, so that I may grow,
close to you in warmth.

An Indian Prayer (Part V)

Great Life giving Spirit,
I face the West,
the direction of the sun down.
Let me remember every day,
that the moment will come,
when my sun will go down.
Never let me forget,
that I must fade into you.
Give me beautiful color.
Give me a great sky for setting,
and when it is time to meet you,
I come with glory.

An Indian Prayer (Part VI)

And giver of all life,
I pray to you from the earth.
Help me to remember
as I touch the Earth
That I am little and need your pity.
Help me to be thankful,
for the Gift of the earth,
and never to walk hurtfully in the world.
Bless and love what comes,
from Mother Earth,
And teach me how to love your gifts.

An Indian Prayer (Part VII)

Great Spirit of the heavens,
Lift me up to you,
that my heart may worship you and
come to you in glory.
Hold in my memory,
that you are my creator,
greater than I,
eager for my good life.
Let everything that is in the world
lift my mind and my heart,
and my love to you,
so that I may always come to you,
in truth and in heart.

Prayer to the Guardian Angel
of a Loved One

Spirit ever watchful,
guardian of thy soul!
May thy pinions carry
my soul's petitioning love,
to the human being upon earth,
Committed to thy care,
united with thy power,
my prayer may radiate with help,
to the soul whom my love is seeking.

Rudolf Steiner

Show Me Your Soul

Show me your soul,
naked of your fear,
and the wounds you,
wear like clothing.
Shed your fear,
your bondage to hurt,
and show me the part of you,
that you hide from me,
fearing that I will reject you.
Let me see all of you,
especially the parts of creativity,
and childlike wonder and joy,
you hid away so many years ago.
Laugh with me,
love with me,
show me your tenderness.
I want to see you free.
Allow me to see you,
your vulnerable spirit,
your great joy and inner beauty,
free of the clutter,
of this world's coverings.

Mark Linden O'Meara

Boundaries

Creator,
help me to know
when to let others help,
and when to ask,
that my boundaries be respected.
Let me steer clear,
of those who would shun me,
because of my pain,
but lead me to those,
who can see the real me,
beyond my troubles.
Show me new ways,
and new behaviours,
thoughts and feelings,
that will lead to new action,
so that I may begin to lean on myself,
instead of others.
Guide me to find,
serenity in myself,
through the teachings of others.

Mark Linden O'Meara

On Leadership

One who leads,
must then be strong and hopeful as the dawn,
that rises unafraid and full of joy,
above the blackness of the darkest night.
One who leads,
must be kind to every living thing;
Kind as the Krishna, Buddha and the Christ,
and full of love for all created life.
Oh, not in war shall great prowess lie,
nor find pleasure in the chase.
Too great for slaughter, friend of man and beast,
touching the borders of the Unseen Realms,
and bringing down to earth their mystic fires,
to light our troubled pathways, wise and kind,
and human to the core,
so shall this leader be,
the coming leader of the coming time.

Adapted from "The Leader to Be"
by Ella Wheeler Wilcox

The Strength
of the Oak

Defeat may serve as well as victory,
to shake the soul and let the glory out.
When the great oak is straining in the wind,
The boughs drink in new beauty,
and the trunk sends down,
a deeper root,
on the windward side.
Only the soul,
that knows the mighty grief,
can know the mighty rapture.
Sorrows come to stretch out,
spaces in the heart,
for joy.

Author unknown

Take Care of Me

Take care of me when I am hungry,
and I will hunger for peace in others.
Take care of me when I am diseased,
and I will be forever grateful.
Take care of me when I am poor,
for when times are better,
I will be generous with others.
Take care of me when I am downtrodden,
and I will be your torch to show others,
that healing can and will be done.

Mark Linden O'Meara

Let Me Earn

Let me earn my solitude,
so that I may find clarity,
of my purpose and self vision.
Let me earn the company of others,
that I may find in them their gifts,
so that I may learn to create,
the luminescent joy of sharing.
Let me earn my living,
and be humble in my skills
so that I may contribute,
to the well being of myself and others.
Let me earn my joy,
so that I may receive,
gifts from my sorrow,
and that I may be,
a friend and companion,
to others on the path.

Mark Linden O'Meara

Hope

I tell you this.
In times of great pain,
do not lose hope!
Remember, you are not defined
by your pain,
and all things eventually pass.
This I promise!
While the times seem dark,
remember that you are loved,
and your soul is valued
by people you may not yet have even met.
Your soul being will arise from the depths.
The soul one that deep down,
knows itself,
free of pain and trauma.
Be diligent in your healing work,
and in some way,
find a lightness in your troubles.
In doing your healing work,
you are burning off,
the karma of many generations,
and clearing the way,
for a better earth.
There is no journey,
more noble and heavenly.

Mark Linden O'Meara

Prayer for Health

God our Creator,
source of all health,
be near those who suffer.
In the time of weakness and pain,
relieve them of their burden,
and heal them,
if it be your will.
Give peaceful sleep to those,
who need rest for soul and body,
and be with them,
in their hours of silence.
Bless those who know not,
what another day will bring.
Make them ready,
for whatever it may be,
whether they must,
stand, sit or be confined.
Grant them a strong spirit,
and inspire with your love,
those who bring,
healing and care to the suffering.
May they bestow your gifts,
of health and strength,
wherever they go.

Traditional Prayer

Forget Me Not

Let no riches make me ever forget myself,
no poverty ever make me to forget thee.
Let no hope or fear, no pleasure or pain,
no accident without, no weakness within,
hinder or discompose my duty,
or turn me from the
ways of thy commandments.
O, let thy Spirit dwell with me forever,
and make my soul just and charitable,
full of honesty, full of religion,
resolute and constant in holy purposes,
but inflexible to evil.
Make me humble and obedient,
peaceable and pious.
Let me never envy any man's goods,
nor deserve to be despised myself,
and if I be, teach me
to bear it with meekness and charity.

Author unknown

Lighting a Candle

I lit a candle,
in the Lord Mayor's Chapel.
I find it hard to know,
what to say,
and to pray,
and I didn't have much time.
But the Light which I offered is,
a little of what I have,
a little of my time,
a little of myself.
I left it burning before the Lord,
before the blessed virgin,
and the whole company of heaven.
The light is a sign of my prayer,
which goes on after I have left,
and of the light of Christ.

from St. Marks Church,
Bristol England

Write Your Name

Write your name,
in kindness, love, and mercy,
on the hearts of those,
who come in contact with you,
and you will never be forgotten.

Thomas Chalmers

Help Me to Know

Help me to know,
when to hold on,
when to work through,
and when to let go,
when to stand up for myself,
and when to walk away,
when to cry and when to laugh,
when to let go of false hope,
and to find hope when there seems none.
And above all, help me to know,
when to have faith,
when it is,
just a silver thread,
to hang on to.

Mark Linden O'Meara

Peace be in the Heart

If peace be in the heart,
the wildest storm is full of solemn beauty,
the midnight flash shows the path of duty,
each living creature tells some new and joyous story,
the very trees and stones all catch a ray of glory,
if peace be in the heart.

Charles Richardson

Fill Your Mind

Fill your mind with positive thoughts,
and there will be no room for negativity.
Fill your days with effective action,
and there will be no room for laziness.
Fill your body with nutritious food,
and there will be no room for toxic junk.
Fill your life with love,
and there will be no room for hate.
Fill your work with challenge,
and there will be no room for discontent.
Fill your heart with goodness,
and there will be no place for evil.
Fill your world with beauty,
and there will be no room for darkness.
Fill your thoughts with peace,
and there will be no room for conflict.
Fill your moves with confidence,
and there will be no room for doubt.
Fill your spirit with abundance,
and there will be no place for distress.
Fill your moments with joy,
and there will be no room for regret.

Ralph Marston

Grant This

Grant that I may love and be loved,
that I see God and good,
in all beings, things and religions,
accepting others as they come before me,
and that I may lose my righteousness,
and claims to truth,
acknowledging the truth in all and all others,
that we may all attain,
heavenhood and enlightenment,
here on earth as it is meant to be.

Author unknown

I Thank My Body

I thank my body
for instinctively knowing,
how to protect myself,
and through the sensations,
alert me to the things in my life,
I needed to learn and heal.
I thank that part of my body,
for its lesson,
and say to those ills, cells and tissue,
that the lesson is learned,
that path of the journey completed,
and the energy is now free to move on,
releasing me to be my true,
loved and loving self,
free to be.

Mark Linden O'Meara

Prayer for Sufferers

Let us pray, for all who suffer,
for the sick and wounded,
for the lonely, fearful and sorrowful,
for those who face the tempest,
of anger, doubt, and despair,
for prisoners and the captive,
both physically, mentally and emotionally,
that the meaning of love,
will comfort and relieve them,
and stir inside all of us,
the will to love and be patient,
and to provide compassion for all in need.

Author unknown

Love is All Around Us

There is love all around us,
like the air we breathe.
It is the space between the atoms,
the water of the creator.
Learn to see it, to feel it,
to bathe yourself in it,
wherever you go,
with whomever you meet.
It is with you at all times,
on your journey of creation,
to feed you, to nurture you,
to hold you.
All you have to do,
is believe,
that it is always here.

Mark Linden O'Meara

In Times of Anger

In times of anger,
and discontent,
gently remind me,
to think with my heart,
and feel with my head.

Mark Linden O'Meara

The Great Center

There is a point of rest,
at the great center of the cyclone's force,
a silence at its secret source,
a little child might slumber undisturbed,
without the ruffle of one fair curl.
In that strange, central calm,
amid the mighty whirl,
it is your business to learn,
to be peaceful and safe,
in God,
in every situation.

Chas Cowman

A Prayer for My Body

Let me listen to the wisdom of my body.
It is a gift from God.
Let me take care of my body,
and love it unconditionally,
accepting what I see as imperfections,
and acknowledging that,
it is perfect for me.
Let me exercise my body,
not in punishment for things overdone,
but to restore and nurture,
my body's vitality and wisdom,
thanking God for its magnificent creation.

Mark Linden O'Meara

Let It Begin With Me

Let words of compassion,
and thoughts of kindness,
and feelings of love,
replace my memories,
of resentment and thoughtlessness.
May my mind become a haven,
for all the good things,
that will transform,
into the courage to love,
those whom I do not understand.
May I bring,
peace and harmony,
to the world.
Let it begin with me.

Mark Linden O'Meara

Harmony

Where there is harmony in the mind,
there will be harmony in the home.
When there is harmony in the home,
there will be harmony in the community.
When there is harmony in the community,
there will be harmony in the county.
When there is harmony in the county,
there will be harmony in the country.
When there is harmony in the country,
there will be harmony in the nations.
When there is harmony in the nations,
there will be harmony in the world.
When there is harmony in the world,
there will be harmony in the mind.
Help me to see that peace,
begins within,
my own mind.

Chinese Proverb

My Highest Service

May my heart be my eyes,
that I may see with clarity.
May my heart be my ears,
that I may hear with understanding.
May my heart be my lips,
that I may speak with compassion.
May my heart be my hands,
that my touch is healing calmness.
May my heart be my mind,
that my thoughts benefit all.
May my heart be my actions,
that truth is accomplished freely.
May my heart be open and at peace,
that I may know my highest experience.
Why judge or limit myself or another,
whose path is unknown,
and dimensions unseen?

John Edwards

My Sanctuary

Help me to find my sanctuary,
in times of trouble, distress and chaos.
May my inner self be nurtured,
consoled and quieted.
When a difficult journey lies ahead,
or the day to day challenges wear me down,
may I continue through these times,
with serenity, hope and faith.
May I be nurtured by my
memory of a quiet place,
where my soul gathers energy,
and replenishes my love,
for myself and those around me.

Mark Linden O'Meara

Prayer to my Teddy Bear

Warm and cuddly,
soft and snuggly,
always be my friend,
as though time will never end.
Hear my prayers,
answer my cares,
to my thoughts please listen,
with your silent eyes that glisten.
Watch over where I play,
think of me when I'm away,
be my friend forever,
tell my secrets never.
Let's escape to Littleland,
with you in my gentle hand.
Play with me and ride in my cart.
Send me kisses, cherish my heart!

Mark Linden O'Meara

Compassion and Forgiveness

I offer these words to myself.
I offer these words to a friend.
I offer these words to a person,
with whom I share tension or conflict:
May you be filled with loving kindness!
May you be well!
May you be peaceful and at ease!
May you be happy!

Author unknown

Commandments of Non-Violence

I live and let live.
I love all. I serve all.
Where there is love there is life.
Violence is suicide.
All souls are alike, and potentially divine.
None is superior or inferior.
All living beings long to live.
No one wants to die.
I have compassion towards all living beings.
Hatred leads to destruction.
I live in the silence,
and self control of non-violence.
Just as I dislike pain,
so all other beings dislike pain.
I am a wise person.
A wise person does not kill,
nor cause others to kill,
nor consent to the killings by others.
Having respect for all living beings is non-violence.
I live in the highest religion of non-violence.

Ahimsa

Goethe's Prayer

Treat people as if they were,
what they ought to be,
and you'll help them to become
what they are capable of becoming.

Goethe

A Prayer to be Heard

Creator, lend me a friend,
one who has faith,
one who will not judge me,
but will listen to hear,
my pain and troubles,
without trying to fix me,
so that I may let go,
and begin to experience,
the joy of your love of creation.

Mark Linden O'Meara

The Immortal Song

May the sacred stream of amity,
flow forever in my heart.
May the universe prosper,
such is my cherished desire.
May my heart sing with ecstasy.
at the sight of the virtuous,
and may my life be,
an offering at their feet.
May my heart bleed,
at the sight of the wretched,
the cruel, the irreligious,
and may tears of compassion,
flow from my eyes.
May I always be there to show,
the path to the pathless,
and the wanderers of life.
Yet if they should not hearken to me,
may I bide in patience.
May the spirit of goodwill,
enter all our hearts.
May we all sing in chorus,
the immortal song,
of human concord.

Jain Prayer

All that Belongs to the Earth

The thoughts of the earth are my thoughts.
The voice of the earth is my voice.
All that belongs to the earth belongs to me.
All that belongs to me belongs to the earth.
All that surrounds the earth surrounds me.
All that surrounds me surrounds the earth.
It is lovely indeed, it is lovely indeed.

Navajo Song

Do All By All

Do all the good you can,
by all the means you can,
in all the ways you can,
in all the places you can,
at all the times you can,
to all the people you can,
as long as ever you can.

John Wesley

My Thought is in Thee

My thought is in Thee,
Inner Light.
My words are from Thee,
Inner Wisdom.
My understanding is of Thee,
Inner God.
I cannot be hid from Thee,
my inspiration and my Life.

Ernest Holmes

The Shepherd

The oriental shepherd,
Was always ahead of his sheep.
He was down in front,
any attack had to take him into account.
Now, God is down in front.
He is in the tomorrows.
All the tomorrows of our life,
must pass through God,
before they can get to us.
God is in every tomorrow,
therefore I live for today,
certain of finding at sunrise,
guidance and strength for the way,
power for each moment of weakness,
hope for each moment of pain,
comfort for every sorrow,
sunshine and joy after rain.

Author unknown

Visiting

Go lightly and simply.
Too much seriousness,
clouds the soul.
Just go,
and follow the flowing moment.
Try not to cling to any experience.
The depths of wonder,
open of themselves.

Frederic Lehrman

Prayer to my Soul Mate

Dear God,
I pray that I may experience,
the fullness of being alone,
yet discover the joy
in being connected with another.
In the many people I meet,
may I discover true joy,
in connecting with a being,
who knows my inner heart,
and who shares my deepest thoughts.
May I overcome my fear,
of such deep intimacy,
and learn to accept this person,
with all their beauty and non-beauty,
and to grow old together,
on separate paths,
that unite in the journey.

Mark Linden O'Meara

God is a Verb

For God to me,
it seems, is a verb,
not a noun, proper or improper;
is the articulation not the art,
objective or subjective;
is loving, not the abstraction "love"
commanded or entreated;
is knowledge dynamic,
not legislative code,
not proclamation law,
not academic dogma,
nor ecclesiastic canon.
Yes, God is a verb, the most active,
connoting the vast harmonic reordering,
of the universe,
from unleashed chaos of energy.
And there is born unheralded
a great natural peace,
not out of exclusive pseudo-static security,
but out of including, refining,
dynamic balancing.
Naught is lost.
Only the false and nonexistent are dispelled.

Buckminster Fuller

The Tapestry

Not until each loom is silent,
and the shuttles cease to fly,
will God unroll the pattern,
and explain the reason why,
the dark threads are as needful,
in the weaver's skillful hand,
as the threads of gold and silver,
for the pattern which God planned.

Author unknown

Clear Mind

Clear mind is like the full moon in the sky.
Sometimes clouds come and cover it,
but the moon is always behind them.
Don't worry about this clear mind.
It is always there.
When thinking comes,
behind it is clear mind.
When thinking goes,
there is always clear mind.

Seung Sahn

My Unspoken Prayers

I asked for riches that I might be happy,
I was given poverty that I might be wise.
I asked for power
that I might have the praise of men,
I was given weakness
that I might feel the need of God.
I asked for all things that I might enjoy life,
I was given life that I might enjoy all things.
Almost despite myself,
my unspoken prayers were answered;
I am, among all people, most richly blessed.

Prayer of an unknown
confederate soldier

With Harmony I Walk

With harmony before me may I walk.
With harmony behind me may I walk.
With harmony above me may I walk.
With harmony underneath my feet, may I walk.
With harmony all around me may I walk.
It is done in harmony.

Navajo Prayer

Prayer for Times
of Adversity

I think over again,
my small adventures, my fears,
those small ones that seemed so big,
for all the vital things,
I had to get and reach.
And yet there is
only one great thing,
the only thing,
to live to see,
the great day that dawns
and the light that fills the world.

An Inuit Prayer

Thanksgiving Prayer

Great and eternal mystery of life,
creator of all things,
I give thanks for the beauty
you put in every single one
of your creations.
I am grateful that you did not fail,
in making every stone, plant, creature,
and human being,
a perfect and whole part,
of the Sacred Hoop.
I am grateful that you have allowed me,
to see the strength and beauty,
of All My Relations.
My humble request,
is that all of the Children of Earth,
will learn to see the same perfection in themselves.
May none of your human children
doubt or question
your wisdom, grace, and sense,
of wholeness in giving all of Creation,
a right to be living extensions,
of your perfect love.

American Indian Prayer

Requirements of Life

We act as though comfort and luxury,
were the chief requirements of life,
when all that we need,
to make us really happy,
is something to be enthusiastic about!

Charles Kingsley

A Personal Creed

Our Creator, who art among us,
hallowed be thy creation.
Thy will be done on earth,
so this may become your heaven.
Provide us with spiritual nourishment,
and forgive us our trespasses
as we forgive those who trespass against us.
Lead us not into temptation
but give us the courage,
to resist hatred and anger,
for love is the kingdom,
the power, and the glory,
forever and ever, Amen.

Author of this adaptation unknown

She Who Heals

Mother, sing me a song,
that will ease my pain,
mend broken bones,
bring wholeness again,
catch my babies when they are born,
sing my death song,
teach me how to mourn,
show me the medicine of the healing herbs,
the value of spirit,
the way I can serve.
Mother, heal my heart
so that I can see the gifts of yours,
that can live through me.

An American Indian Healing Prayer

Prayer for Peace

Lead me from death to life,
from falsehood to truth.
Lead me from despair to hope,
from fear to trust.
Lead me from hate to love,
from war to peace.
Let peace fill our heart,
our world, our universe.

Jain Prayer

Giving Thanks

For the precious things of heaven,
the stars, the sunsets,
the clouds and even the storms,
we thank thee, Lord.
For dew sparkling in the sunshine,
the deeps of the ocean,
and the stillness of little pools,
we thank thee, Lord.
For the wealth of crops from the sunlight,
and the wealth of produce month by month,
the beauty and the bounty of growing things,
the verdant and the fertile land,
we thank thee Lord.
For the chief things of the ancient mountains,
and the precious things of the lasting hills,
majesty, serenity, power,
we thank thee Lord.
For the brilliancy of mind,
good will and love that radiates from friends,
We thank thee Lord.

Otis Moore

Prayer for Pardon

Forgive me most gracious Lord,
if this day I have done or said anything,
to increase the pain of the world.
Pardon the unkind word, the impatient gesture,
the hard and selfish deed,
the failure to show sympathy and kindly help,
where I have had the opportunity but missed it,
and enable me so to live,
that I may daily do something,
to lessen the tide of human sorrow,
and to add to the sum of human happiness.

Author unknown

Peace I Leave You

Peace I leave with you,
my peace I give unto you,
not as the world giveth,
give I unto you.
Let not your heart be troubled,
neither let it be afraid.

John 14:27

A Voyageur Prayer

Be the canoe that holds me in the sea of life.
Be the steer that keeps me straight.
Be the outrigger that supports me,
in times of great temptation.
Let thy spirit be my sail,
that carries me through each day.
Keep my body strong,
so that I may paddle steadfastly on,
in the long voyage of life.

A Hebridean Prayer

My Crown

My crown is in my heart,
not on my head,
not decked with diamonds,
and Indian stones.
Nor to be seen,
my crown is called content.
A crown it is,
that seldom kings enjoy.

William Shakespeare

Help for Chronic Pain

While I pray for a miracle,
that my pain will go away,
I acknowledge that life itself,
often involves suffering.
This pain is difficult to bear
without getting angry,
resentful or discouraged.
Help me to find the tools and support
to maintain a sense of focus,
to notice the good things,
to accept the difficult,
to acknowledge but not complain,
to accelerate my thoughts of peace,
and to train my mind to love,
the part of me that hurts.
May I be granted the ability,
to acknowledge my pain and not deny it,
to ask for help when I need it,
and to spend time,
with You each morning,
to prepare for my day ahead,
and to thank you at day's end.

Mark Linden O'Meara

Prayer of Surrender

Help me to admit,
that this problem,
is greater than me alone.
I cannot solve it in the milieu that created it.
Help me to turn this problem over to you,
and release my need to control.
Help me to get out of my own way,
to let go and let you do your work.
I give up this problem into your hands,
asking for your guidance,
and that at the appointed hour,
according to your plan,
release me into your solution.

Mark Linden O'Meara

Relaxation

May I think of a word,
that helps me stay centered,
to focus on good,
to focus on greatness,
to maintain forward movement,
to remain compassionate.
Let this word resound,
through my mind, body, and spirit,
to be called forth,
to remind me,
of this feeling,
whenever I need your presence.
May the word be love.

Mark Linden O'Meara

Prayer for the Unity of All Life

May the winds, the oceans, the herbs,
and night and days, the mother earth,
the father heaven, all vegetation,
and the sun be all sweet to us.
Let us follow the path of goodness,
for all times, like the sun and the moon,
moving eternally in the sky.
Let us be charitable to one another.
Let us not kill,
or be violent with one another.
Let us know and appreciate,
the points of view of others.
And let us unite.
May the God who is friendly,
benevolent, all-encompassing,
measurer of everything,
the sovereign, the lord of speech,
may God shower blessings on us.
Oh Lord, remove my indiscretion
and arrogance, control my mind.
Put an end to the snare,
of endless desires.
Broaden the sphere of compassion,
and help me to cross,
the ocean of existence.

Hindu Prayer

Prayer of Saint Francis

Where there is charity and wisdom,
there is neither fear nor ignorance.
Where there is patience and humility,
there is neither anger nor vexation.
Where there is poverty and joy,
there is neither greed nor avarice.
Where there is peace and meditation,
there is neither anxiety nor doubt.

Saint Francis of Assisi

An Irish Prayer of Blessing

May the road rise to meet you,
may the wind be always at your back,
may the sun shine warm on your face,
the rain fall softly on your fields;
and until we meet again,
may God hold you,
in the palm of God's hand.

Gaelic Prayer for
Saint Patrick's Day

Unconditional Guidance

Dear Creator,
I know that you care,
and that you love me,
when I am following your path,
And when I am not.
I know that you will nudge me,
into your divine plan,
that you have created for me.
I know that you will not judge me unfairly,
when I make mistakes.
Guide me in your truth,
to find my way,
to be cradled in your heart.

Author unknown

Shining Words

The joy of the Lord is your strength.
God in me is infinite wisdom,
showing me what to do.
In all thy ways acknowledge him,
and he will direct thy path.
I can do all things through Christ,
which strengthen me.
Naught can disturb me,
for Christ is my peace and my poise.
All things work together for good.
In quietness and in confidence,
God shall be my strength.
Faith is the strength of the soul inside,
and lost is the person without it.
The greatest teaching ever given
is Christ in you, the hope of glory.
God is my help in every need.

Favorite affirmations
of Charles Fillmore

Dreamland

How far to Dreamland?
Every baby knows.
The road leads straight through mother's arms.
You follow it safe from all alarms.
She holds you warm and close.
What does one see in dreamland?
Every baby knows.
The things she promised as you crept
on to her lap before you slept -
all the delights you chose.
What does one do in dreamland?
Laugh and sing and play.
Never a soul says "don't" to you.
There isn't a thing you mustn't do,
the happy, livelong day.

Juliet Bredon

Letting Go

Beloved Creator,
I pray to thee that I will understand,
all that I do not understand,
and let go of traditions and beliefs,
that do not create harmony and love,
for all human beings.
The Creator knows,
that this is difficult for me,
but the Creator helps me to love everyone.

Mark Linden O'Meara

Creating the Thoughts

May I have a song of joy,
a glimmer of hope,
a gentle word,
and a tender heart,
a star to wish upon,
and a friend within.
May I have all of these things,
that cannot be seen,
cannot be bought,
but can always be created,
with just one thought!

Mark Linden O'Meara

Your Children

Your children are not your children.
They are the sons and daughters,
of Life's longing for itself.
They come through you,
but not from you,
and though they are with you,
yet they belong not to you.
You may give them your love,
but not your thoughts,
for they have their own thoughts.
You may house their bodies,
but not their souls,
for their souls
dwell in the house of tomorrow,
which you cannot visit,
not even in your dreams.
You may strive to be like them,
but seek not to make them like you,
for life goes not backward,
nor tarries with yesterday.
You are the bows,
from which your children,
as living arrows,
are sent forth.

Kahlil Gibran

Prayer for the End of the Day

The day, with the work God gave me to do,
is done and now the night has come,
quiet and calm and beautiful.
As shadows gather around the earth,
I will trust myself, body and spirit,
into God's loving tender care and go to sleep.
God's love is all around me,
and as flood tides from the ocean,
fill each cranny of the bay,
so power and peace from God,
can fill my life as I rest quietly. Amen.

Albert W Palmer (adaptation)

Spiritual Light is Shining

Let Thy spiritual light,
shine upon my body,
and illumine my heart.
Baptize me with Thy sweet dew,
so that it may wash away,
all stains of hatred and ill-will,
cleanse me from all sin and foulness,
and make me pure in thought and deed.
Guard me both day and night from all evil.
Be ever with me, O Pusa,
when I wake and when I sleep.
Grant that my understanding may awaken,
under the rays of Thy glory.
Grant that I may increase,
in spiritual intelligence and discernment.

Buddhist Prayer

Blessed Lord's Song

He who hates no creature
and is friendly and compassionate to all,
who is free from attachment and egotism,
equal-minded in pleasure and pain,
and forgiving. . .
he is dear to me.

From The Blessed Lord's Song
- The Bhagavad-Gita (the Song of God)

A Long Life

Guide not the hand of God,
nor order the finger of the Almighty,
unto thy will and pleasure.
Be able to be alone.
Lose not the advantage of solitude,
and the society of thyself.
If length of days be thy portion,
make it not thy expectation.
Reckon not upon a long life:
Think every day the last,
and live always beyond thy account.
He that so often surviveth his expectations,
lives many lives.

Sir Thomas Browne

On Work

Blessed is he who has found his work;
Let him ask no other blessedness.
He has a work,
a life-purpose,
he has found it and will follow it.

Thomas Carlyle

Song of My Life

Lord of power, Lord of might.
God and Creator of us all,
Lord of day and Lord of night,
listen to our solemn call
listen, whilst to thee we raise
songs of prayer, and songs of praise.
Light, and love, and life are thine.
Great Creator of all good!
Fill our souls with light divine;
Give us with our daily food
blessing from thy heavenly store,
blessing rich for evermore.
Graft within our heart of hearts,
love undying for thy name;
Bud us ere the day departs,
spread afar our maker's fame;
Young and old together bless,
clothe our soul with righteousness.
Full of years, and full of peace,
may our life on earth be blest;
When our trials here shall cease,
and at least we sink to rest,
fountain of eternal love,
call us to our home above!

Godfrey Thring

201

Breath of God

Breathe on me, Breath of God,
fill me with life anew,
that I may love what thou dost love,
and do what thou wouldst do.
Breathe on me, Breath of God,
until my heart is pure,
until with thee I will one will,
to do or to endure.
Breathe on me, Breath of God,
till I am wholly thine,
till all this earthly part of me,
glows with thy fire divine.
Breathe on me, Breath of God,
so shall I never die,
but live with thee the perfect life,
of Thine eternity.

Edwin Hatch

Hand in Hand

Hand in hand with angels,
through the world we go;
Brighter eyes are on us
than we blind ones know.
Tender voices cheer us
than we deaf will own;
Never, walking heavenward,
can we walk alone.
Hand in hand with angels,
some are out of sight,
leading us, unknowing,
into paths of light.

Lucy Laroom

Counting

Count your blessings instead of your crosses.
Count your gains instead of your losses.
Count your joys instead of your woes.
Count your smiles instead of your tears.
Count your courage instead of your fears.
Count your health instead of your wealth.
Count on God instead of yourself.

Author unknown

Becoming

I become self-harmonized,
because the mind,
does nothing.
I become self-regulated,
because the mind,
loves quietude.
I become rich,
because the mind,
enjoys leisure.
I become clear,
because the mind,
has few desires.

Author unknown

Safely Home

I am home in Heaven, dear ones.
Oh, so happy and so bright!
There is perfect joy and beauty
in this everlasting light.
All the pain and grief is over,
every restless tossing passed;
I am now at peace forever,
safely home in Heaven at last.
Did you wonder why I so calmly
trod the valley of the shade?
Oh but God's love illumined
every dark and fearful glade
and God came beside to meet me
in that way so hard to tread;
And with God's arm to lean on
could I have doubt or dread.
Then you must not grieve so sorely,
For I love you dearly still;
Try to look beyond earth's shadows,
pray to trust our Creator's Will.
There is work still waiting for you,
so you must not idly stand:
do it now, while life remaineth
you shall rest in God's land.
When that work is all completed,
you will be gently called to heaven.
Oh, the rapture of that meeting,
Oh, the joy to see you again!

Author unknown

Imitating our Lord

May I nurture a humble opinion of myself,
be united with you in my heart,
be prudent in what I accept and do,
avoid false confidence and arrogance,
resist the temptation of hasty judgment,
bear the defects of others with patience,
to know when to be led and when to be a leader,
to open my heart to forgiveness and gratitude,
to feel the joy of pure consciousness,
and the pure love of God.

Mark Linden O'Meara
inspired by the
Imitation of Christ
by Thomas Kempis

On Awakening

Thank you Lord
for giving me life and health.
Fill my heart with love,
and give me the strength to do your will,
so that all my actions,
may be in your name,
and for your glory.

Author unknown

Wanderer's Song

The golden Sun is my lover,
The silver Moon is my friend,
The clouds are my boon companions
from dawn until daylight's end.
I would rather follow the eagle,
or the wild geese, flying free,
I would rather chum with the mountains,
or hark to the roar of the sea.

Juliet Bredon

Grant Protection and Goodness

Grant, God, thy refuge;
and in refuge, strength;
and in strength, understanding;
and in understanding, knowledge;
and from knowledge, knowledge of what is right;
and from knowledge of what is right, the love of it;
and from loving, the love of God and all goodness.

A Druid Prayer

I Surrender my Soul

Lord, I give up my own purposes and plans,
all my own desires, hopes and ambitions,
and accept Thy will for my life.
I give myself, my life, my all,
utterly to Thee,
to be Thine forever.
I hand over to Thy keeping,
all of my friendships and my love.
Fill me and seal me with Thy Holy Spirit.
Work out Thy whole will in my life,
at any cost, now and forever.

Elizabeth Alden Scott

Illumination

During the moment of illumination,
when I see the original face of mind,
A limitless compassion ariseth.
The greater the illumination,
the greater is the compassion.
The greater my compassion,
the deeper is the wisdom I feel.
The unmistakable path of two-in-one,
is the peerless practice of the Dharma.

The Words of Garmaba,
in the Vow of Mahamudra

Guide Me on The Path

If there be heresy or error in my speech,
I pray that Thee will kindly pardon it,
and set me then upon the Righteous Path.
Lord., from the sun-orb of Thy grace,
the radiant rays of light have shone,
and opened wide,
the petals of the Lotus of my heart,
So that it breatheth forth,
the fragrance born of knowledge,
for which I am for ever bounden unto Thee;
So will I worship Thee by constant meditation.
Vouchsafe to bless me in mine efforts,
that good may come,
to every sentient being.
Lastly, I ask forgiveness too,
for any lavishness of words

From the Biography of Jetsun-Kahbum
according to the late Lama Kazi Dawa-Samdup

Nirvana

One little unforgotten, mortal day,
I shall slip off my body like a garment,
and soar away, quite light and free,
to enter Thee, O Everlasting Peace!
And they deep Night,
splashed by a thousand suns,
will drown my small desire
for Earth and home and Self.

Juliet Bredon

As I Walk

The universe is walking with me.
In beauty it walks before me.
In beauty it walks behind me.
In beauty it walks below me.
In beauty it walks above me.
Beauty is on every side.
As I walk, I walk with Beauty.

Traditional Navajo Prayer

This Universe

This universe, wondrous and infinite,
O Lord, is Thy handiwork;
And the whole world is a treasure-house,
full of Thy beauty and grace.
The stars glisten innumerable,
like gems on a myriad suns and moons
ever be numbered above?
The earth is glowing with grain and gold,
Thine ever brimming store;
Uncounted stars, O God, sing forth;
blessed, blessed art Thou!

Excerpt from The Gospel of
Sri Ramakrishna

All May Be

May all be fed.
May all be healed.
May all be loved.

John Robbins

9 780968 045992